ANCHOR BOOKS

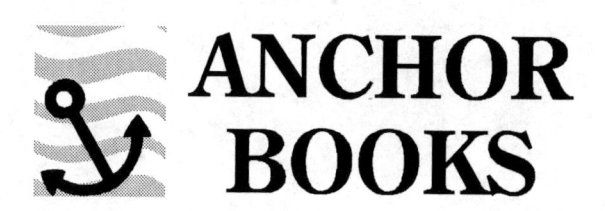

POETS FROM LONDON & HOME COUNTIES 1998

Edited by

Heather Killingray

First published in Great Britain in 1998 by
ANCHOR BOOKS
1-2 Wainman Road, Woodston,
Peterborough, PE2 7BU
Telephone (01733) 230761

All Rights Reserved

Copyright Contributors 1998

HB ISBN 1 85930 626 8
SB ISBN 1 85930 621 7

FOREWORD

Anchor Books is a small press, established in 1992, with the aim of promoting readable poetry to as wide an audience as possible.

We hope to establish an outlet for writers of poetry who may have struggled to see their work in print.

The poems presented here have been selected from many entries. Editing proved to be a difficult task and as the Editor, the final selection was mine.

Poets from London & Home Counties 1998 is a compilation of poems written from poets who reside in London and the Home Counties.

The poems within this anthology reach out to the reader and reveal a reflective and unique portrayal of everyday issues and occurrences. The subjects range from scenes of the countryside to poems about loved ones, how they react to whatever life throws at them. It's all here in black and white. So why not read on and find out how the poets' minds work, read about their perceptions of life and this collection will no doubt leave you riveted for ages.

I trust this selection will delight and please the authors and all those who enjoy reading poetry.

Heather Killingray
Editor

CONTENTS

A Love Poem	Y L D Mullins	1
Oh, How I Love to Lie	George Taylor	2
Love Match	J E Chalkley	3
I Wish! I Wish!	Ann Sandwil	4
The Kiss	Rene McDermott	5
The Perfect Day	L Fulker	6
I'll Be There	Mohsin Malik	7
Passing By	Allen Jessop	8
Wordsmithery	Brian Groves	9
Untitled	Jill Truman	10
A Missed Lifetime . . .	Rosetta Williams	11
The Girlfriend	Claire Murray	12
Reality	Kay Osmond	13
Don't Draw On The Window	Frankie M Rogers	14
Wandle	Margaret Avis	15
The Emigrant	B Haycock	16
To A Daughter In Hospital	Ivy Russell	17
Our Love Is Immortal	Roy Baker	18
Life Is A Gift	Leigh Laniyan	19
Visions	Frances Falvey	20
Welcome Back	Rosylee Bennett	21
Sleeping Rough	M Crickmore	22
Apple Tree	C H Locke	23
On Viewing The Quick And The Dead	Pascale Pollier	24
Gangsta Culture	Denis Parratt	25
Streatham Now	W Fred Tabaczynski	26
The Weeping Willow	Sandra Brisck	27
The King	George Dickens	28
Thoughs Of London	Maria Driffill	29
Only	Nicola Millwood	30
One	Anna Heffron	31
Therapy	Fran Pulford	32
The Tramp With Sparkly Eyes	T L Kelvie	33
At A Glance	Mischa Pearlman	34

Memories	Sally Copeland	35
In The Aftermath	James Grieve	36
Isle Of Sheppey	F E M Grimwade	37
The Veterinary Visit	I Ayres	38
The Blue Poppy Effect	Amanda Ritson	39
My Blessings	Penny	40
Leysdown On Sea	R E J Gent	41
Battle Stations	Mark Tann	42
Reasons To Be Happy	Sally Carpenter	43
Just As Before	Howard Lucas	44
Emily	David Hallwood	45
Unknown Regions	Una Daniels	46
Last Love	Tony Skidmore	47
Streetwise Woman	Shaun Edwards	48
Dedicated To My Husband	D Sampford	49
Gentle April Breeze	Richard Francis	50
The Violent Sea	D H Pepperrell	51
Hatfield Heath	David Brown	52
Follow Me	Rachel Wake	53
Fairies	Jane Bye	54
I Am	S Went	55
An I Am Poem	Emma Cass	56
Heaven And Earth	Jennifer Vrahimis	57
Our Men In The Gate	J A Taft	58
Inside St Thomas' Gate	Donald James Munday	59
Lines Written In Memory Of A Proposal	C F Iggulden	60
The Reluctant Gardener	David John Gaywood	61
Sounds In The Silence	Brian Frost	62
I'd Like To Be A Kitten!	Jenny Lines	63
Just For Now	Patrick Farrelly	64
The Lesson	Helen Tingley	65
Dying Love	Samantha Gout	66
Valentine For Charlie	S F Burley	67
Untitled	Martin Harris Parry	68
Memories	Maggie Ford	69
Spring Song	Geraldine Foy	70
Cursed With A Minor Talent	Vic Lime	71

Dark Rooms	K McDonagh	72
Your Valentine?	SQ	73
The Change Of Time	Minnie Dann	74
Elemental Experience (Water, Fire, Air And Earth)	Janis Huntley	75
Deep Loss	Elaine Coldwell	76
Untitled	S Wickes	77
Shattered Dream	Linda Walker	78
Duty Calls	Robert Wassell	79
My Dream	Enzo Gizzi	80
Not Long To Live?	Tristan Cooper	81
A Man Who Loved Women	Lesley Gooden	82
Ode To The Bung	John Gooden	83
Summer's Gone Terry	Sheila Rabbetts	84
Paradox	Barbara Anslow	85
Breathing	Keith Donachie	86
War Poem	Andrea Foulkes	88
'Honey's' Coming Home	Terry	89
Hallowe'en?	Charlie Keenan	90
Having Known You From Afar	Mark Dunn	91
The Dress	Helen Cronin	92
Atlas In A Suit	Leigh Hunt	93
Barbed Wired Hard Drive	J A Gill	94
Hope	Sue Calvert	95
The Now	C Leith	96
Colour Of Day	Christine Ashworth	97
The Old Wall	T J Martin	98
Just A Word In Passing	E Fisher	99
Diminishing Hope	Ghazala Rashid	100
Where Is My Heart?	Ruth M Davies	101
Sunday Peace	Olive Martin	102
Simple Pleasures	Kate Smith	103
To Jane	Barbara Jane Richardson	104
Bird	Archie Wilson	105
Our Eden	William Hudson-Jones	106
Death Visits	Belinda Lonie	107

A Love Poem

Do you think of me -
At all?
Is love ever unbesieged by trauma?
Ever a joy?
It never is for me.
Can one ever tell or read the signs
That the seed of love is planted in another's heart?
This cerebral wordless love-filled craving -
Which has torn my life apart.

I love you dearly.
And dearly would I like to know - for sure
If you love me?
Do I imagine all the singing of the stars
When you speak to me alone!
The times when seeing you -
The world becomes our own cocoon.
No I don't!
But what of you?

Do I take it all too seriously
In a maudlin melancholy way?
What is this love - a devil's lair?
Then I should cast this millstone far away from me!
Begging - flee love flee!
For all I know the one I love
Makes fun of me!
But stubborn heart
My love's too strong to leave.

Y L D Mullins

OH, HOW I LOVE TO LIE
(Sonnet for an aged dreamer)

Oh, how I love to lie abed with her,
And she, in apposition, lie with me.
Summit of lustful love; we twain concur.
No words describe this height of ecstasy.
And then with passion mutually spent,
Lie, locked together, hand entwined in hand;
Eyes, looking into eyes, with gaze intent,
Each other's very soul to understand.
Then deep slumber, joy of love's fulfilling.
Time to replenish; stoke the lover's fuel.
Whether she or me this tale is telling,
Think carefully on't for our deceit is cruel.
  For she is ninety. I am ninety three.
  Which one of us the great liar be?

George Taylor

Love Match

Just one more chance of happiness to reap
Promises this time always for keeps
And endless journey for the everlasting kiss
Hold together tight, a locked in bliss.

Bright light flooding our love again
Casting such colour, a beautiful end
So lost in our love, always we touch
Fading to the distance with the wonder of lust.

Your Junoesque features, elegant and strong
Was it up to fate to make us belong?
Those soothing eyes and feeling at peace
I want to scream in this happy release.

There's no advice on how to make love work
As people change in the relationship curve
To be strong for each other and able to listen
Hardens the coat, holds onto the vision.

Many still wander, isolation seems home
Happy with themselves, so secure when alone
Shuddering thoughts revealing so much
In this tragic parade of broken-down love.

J E Chalkley

I Wish! I Wish!

I wish I hadn't left him.
I thought he'd make me stay.
I wish I'd thought of us - not me
Had heard my heart - not felt my feet.

He loved me so, I knew it then.
Brought out my inner self with love.
He changed my hair, my face and dress.

The passing years taught me to wait -
To try the options, talk and think.
I wish we'd talked things over then.

I loved him then - I love him now
I wish, I wish I had him still!

Ann Sandwil

THE KISS

Ah, yes, I remember it well Mum,
   the day that our dad went away.
You gathered us children together,
   and told us to go out to play.

You said when you finished your breakfast,
   you would come out and join in our game.
Then we'd all catch a bus to the station,
   Where Daddy would get on a train.

Well, we all had a peep through the window,
   there was Carry, and Bobby, and me.
And though we were watching you closely,
   it was clear that you just didn't see.

For, as you reached out for the teapot,
   majestically poised on the stand.
Daddy caught hold of your fingers,
   and planted a kiss on your hand.

Then we all made our way to the station,
   and we ardently waved him goodbye.
In his uniform he looked so handsome,
   that I thought you were silly to cry.

Well, he never came back from the war Mum,
   and I never did quite understand.
But whenever you reach for the teapot,
   I can still see his kiss on your hand.

Rene McDermott

THE PERFECT DAY

And at the end of the perfect day, dear
When your hair has turned to grey
And the children have all left home dear
And there's nothing left to say.

At the end of the perfect day dear
When the sun's o'er the brow of the hill,
You will look in my eyes and know dear
That yes, I love you still.

When we've lived and loved a long time dear,
And there's nothing left to do
At the end of the perfect day, dear
There'll still be me, and you.

L Fulker

I'll Be There

With every word you say,
I'll be there,
With every sound you hear,
I'll be there,
With every sight you see,
I'll be there,
With every thought you think,
I'll be there,
With every breath you take,
I'll be there,
Because I care,
And whether as lovers or as friends,
We'll always get through,
Because I will always, always love you.

Mohsin Malik

PASSING BY

When your carpet slippers beckon rather than your running shoes
And the deck chair's more inviting than listening to the sports news,
The years are passing by!

When you'd rather go to bed with a book in your hand
To read of a journey to some far distant land,
The years are passing by!

When people look surprised to find you're still around
You know they're thinking 'I thought he'd be in the ground,'
The years are passing by!

If you think *Oasis* is a welcoming water hole
And your state pension is your next exciting goal,
The years are passing by!

When the obituary columns look like a list of friends
And you realise their journeys have come to their respective ends,

The years are passing by!
When your grandchildren ask for the key of the door
It dawns on you finally that they are now mature,
The years are passing by!

When you open your eyes at the start of each new day
You feel thankful to have been granted a stay
And that life has not yet passed you by!

Allen Jessop

WORDSMITHERY

Noah! did he know her?
The triad did try hard
The sloe its growth was slower
And Stratford barred the bard

The poles went to the polls
Keys opened Surrey Quays
Cole's pipe was lit with coals
And feys sometimes charged fees

Wearing a ruff could be rough
A maid was made but seldom laid
A tuff was, is and can be tough
The virgin staid a virgin stayed

Never laze upon the leys
Far off one can see the sea
Do not craze to use the crays
Or to be a bee or not to be

Bus trips sometimes make bees buzz
Though the fly prefers the phalli
Both at times do fuss the fuzz
But both would rather dye than die

Brian Groves

UNTITLED

O ver the hill? No way. We
L ove life the more as it ebbs,
D aring at last to be ourselves.

Jill Truman

A Missed Lifetime...
(To dearest Rosana... with a sister's love... for eternity)

She took a wrong train,
Arrived in the wrong lifetime, in pain.
Stayed nearly thirty-nine years, in sadness.
Searching for the way out...out of the madness.
A rose planted in a bad garden,
Helpless in the lions' den.
Too little love; too little water;
Too much pain. Ah! but now it doesn't matter.
Now the rose has gone home.
Now, there is water aplenty. Now she is no more alone.
Left behind, another rose, missing a sister's love.
Yet, knowing she is never far; watching from above.
Sleep now, little one. A son still lives.
Much joy and love he always gives.
A part of you; a part of me;
All this, our earthly world to see!

Rosetta Williams

THE GIRLFRIEND

I love the way you look tonight,
Your eyes are such a wonderful sight,
You are the one I love,
Your face is as white as a dove.

You look so lovely in a dress of lace,
And the pale white of your face,
I miss you so much when you go away,
But you have come back to me today.

Your lips are red like a rose,
And with your perfect nose,
Your hair is charcoal black,
You are the one I lack.

Your teeth are so white,
They shine like a light,
Your eyes are so blue,
I love you and I need you.

Claire Murray

REALITY

Solitary confinement, not on your own
In a town full of people, unknown.
Friends and people you see, lonely
Faces around, yet there is only you.

On your own, yet life has its pleasures
No noise or movement, but many treasures.
No faces or crowds, yet feeling befriended
Happy and content when day has ended.

Such different worlds, so small, so far
All feeling the same wherever we are
Lonely amongst so many.
Happy with so few.

Kay Osmond

DON'T DRAW ON THE WINDOW!

There was a steamed up window,
Perfect for the deed,
As the dainty digit traced,
The words for mum to read.

On misty pane the fingers glide,
A work of art creating,
As performers on the ice,
Her dancing digits skating.

How fast fades the steamy slate,
And on it what was drawn,
But not in time to save her from
The tongue of mother's scorn.

With a sense of deja vu
My daughter here I see,
But not so many years ago
That erring child was me!

My mum however did not scold,
But sighed with resignation.
She couldn't curb artistic flare,
Nor window decoration.

After all those windows will
The same space occupy,
As evidence of little hands,
Is lost as time goes by.

Now the sun through window glares
And no harm has been done,
As the image re-appears,
It reads 'I love you, mum.'

Frankie M Rogers

WANDLE

Over stone and wet moist ground,
Silently but noisily I move around.
Fields and buildings I pass by
Dragonflies skim my sky
Here's a bridge that I can see,
Grassy bank, branch of tree.

Once a mighty wheel did move,
Grain to grind,
Power to prove,
Now no longer makes a sound,
As my life is onward bound.

Times have changed, so have I,
Now I see, in my sky
Car, train, plane and different dress,
My life's blood clogged with plastic mess.

But I still feel the touch,
Of the past, so very much.
History I have seen,
Monks, kings and queens.
My banks have blessed
Staid and royally dressed.

Children my skies do shatter,
Skimming stone, noisy chatter.
Swans regally dip their beak,
Poets and fishers silence seek.
Do not let me go to ground
For I must always move around.
Water is the blood of life,
Keep me clean and free from strife.

Margaret Avis

THE EMIGRANT

Stay thy soft, and trembling lips,
Shed not your tears for me,
Though my dearth, bring pain to you,
My spirit still, be there with thee.

Think not of me, forever lost,
But as a joyous pilgrim gone,
In search of fertile land afar,
A home anew, to build upon.

Keep to your breast, our son, my heir,
Suppress all fear in one so young,
His eyes one day, this letter show,
And teach him in his father's tongue.

Liken not oneself, to a soul cast out,
As flotsam on the open sea,
But rich in harvest, mind content,
In knowledge of my love for thee.

As each day dawn, e're evening fall,
And seasons come and go,
Together, we again will be,
Loves bond, will make this so.

B Haycock

TO A DAUGHTER IN HOSPITAL

God send you back to me soon, my dear,
home has no meaning without you.
No heaps of paper on the table and chairs,
no piles of books on the carpet upstairs,
no left-off shoes in the corners - who cares?
Home is a place for unwinding.

   God send you back to me soon, my dear,
   home lacks enjoyment without you.
   'Granny Smith apples again? What a bore!
   Don't you know strawberries are in the store?
   Pink melons too, and they're gorgeous, what's more.'
   Home is a good place for learning.

God send you back to me soon, my dear,
something is missing without you.
Coming home late from an outing, 'night-night!'
whispers a voice by my bedroom. 'Sleep tight!'
Somebody cares, and my dreams are all bright.
God send you back to me soon.

Ivy Russell

OUR LOVE IS IMMORTAL

So still the waters of my heart,
that raged so fierce when we must part.
Still my life when once it flowed,
for pity's sake life let me go.

Who comes with knock on door,
dark angel protect me more.
Stand at threshold shield in hand,
may darkness fall where this place stand.

Within that darkness still as death,
send her to me, give her breath.
Give her voice that she may speak,
also hand to touch my cheek.

Just this once I thee implore,
just this time I ask no more.
To walk again hand in hand,
on this sweet earth in this fair land.

Roy Baker

Life Is A Gift

Everybody's life is a gift,
Don't let your dreams go adrift.
Just get in your lift and go right to the top . . .
And just don't stop.
So get the most out of your life.
Always do your best,
And when you do, you'll always feel good . . .
About yourself, like you always should.
You always have to thrive
To stay alive.

Leigh Laniyan

VISIONS

I watched the sun arise from earth,
And give the day a new re-birth.
The rosebuds raised their drooping heads,
A magic stirred the flower beds.

The dewdrops sparkled in the sun,
The songbirds wakened one by one.
Their chorus started sweet and low,
And soon became a crescendo.

As mother nature paves the way
To help the earth to a grand new day.
So are *we* given the chance to renew
The strength and the courage to see the day through.

We can rise up in the freshness of dawn,
And start a new day knowing we are re-born.
Bathed in the strength of the warmth of the sun,
And raise our bowed heads -a new day has begun.

Dawn lifts the darkness of night . . . and despair,
The anguish and hopelessness no longer there.
Like the flowers raising their heads to the sun,
We can rise up to a new day begun.

Frances Falvey

WELCOME BACK

'Welcome back', the Saviour said, 'you've been away so long.
My love for you remains unchanged whatever you did wrong.
Your weakness I can turn around, in sorrow I can make you smile,
There's nothing I won't do for you
My Child! My Child! My Child!'

Oh Lord, there were so many times I struggled just to cope,
I stumbled from one day to next completely without hope . . .
And then I heard You calling, 'Come' when I could take no more;
And in my hand You placed the key, and I unlocked the door.

'Welcome back!' the Saviour said, whilst you had gone away,
Not once did I stop loving you with every passing day.
My love burned brightly like a flame, held high for you to see
The path ahead, so you could find your way back home to me.'

O Lord, I wandered far from You, and I learnt to my cost,
The moment I released Your hand all joy in life was lost,
I tried but failed so many times, my pride was much to blame,
But then I heard You calling me, and I was filled with shame.

'O Child, how much I've longed to hear you call to Me, invite Me in.
I've waited just to hear you say, 'Lord cleanse me from my sin.'
Hush child, don't cry; it's finished, come into My arms where
you belong,
The past is just a memory, and I will make you strong.'

In looking back I see the signs that turned my life around.
And slowly every step I take leads back to solid ground.
Now that I'm safely in Your arms, one thing I must convey,
How good it feels, to know that I am in Your arms to stay.

'Oh Child! Oh Child!'

Rosylee Bennett

SLEEPING ROUGH

London streets, are not paved with gold,
If you think that it is, just so,
When you arrive, everything is strange,
And you are left out, in the cold.

First, you look for a job, with no luck,
Then, no rooms if you have no cash,
No help, if you have no address,
So think on, don't be rash.

Try and sort out, your troubles at home.
Stick with your mum and dad,
Because, sleeping rough, no job, no money,
Is really, really bad!

M Crickmore

APPLE TREE

An apple tree grows in my head
and fruits games which we used to play
in that garden, my mother's garden,
a girl's garden then
and now.

I can taste in my mind the sweetness
of just plucked juice, how it ran
down my mouth and still runs
sweet as I think it.

That gnarled old tree still claws
at memory and will not let go. I can see
myself, a girl, a girl in a tree,
laughing at sisters' antics, brothers' swinging,
like a monkey, far below.
But not too far below. Always at hand.

A red, creaky swing whose hinges
were yanked from the ground by girls
taking flight, high into the upper blue,
and the canopy of the tree, above.

The tree was love, I know it now,
the tree was a love we needed,
a love we knew.

C H Locke

ON VIEWING THE QUICK AND THE DEAD

Mortal flesh and bone with benign fleeting soul
composed grief-stricken structure
i doth require your disengaged frame, your relinquished mould
before this beautiful perfection mingles moist turf and oak
and throwes of graveyard soil
Many brights have wrought
and eyed upon thee
and chalked eternal masterworks from thee
bequeath therefore your strange intriguing tenements of clay
to medic shaman and artist
and behold
an absolute awaits

Pascale Pollier

GANGSTA CULTURE

The rancid air that left him there
The decomposing body bare
Another hit Chicago fashion
Beaten down by barbed-wire passion.

The acrid stench of life devoid
Gives credence to a soul destroyed
As willing flesh returns to flower
Death becomes the witching hour.

The pungent taste of death vacates
The lifeless body lain to waste
As circumstances know for certain
Greed brought down the final curtain.

Denis Parratt

STREATHAM NOW

Streatham is a fine interesting place,
With a mixture of many a race.
It has many abroad, good road,
Where car drivers obey the Highway Code.
There are two large, green parks,
Where early one can hear the larks.
The shops sell many a varied thing,
And one can buy all that money can bring.
The houses are of good quality,
And worth investment to beat off poverty.
The law and the policeman Bobbie,
Are welcome as are the ambulance man Robbie.
It has three railway stations,
Which help London's communications.
There is an ice-rink and two cinemas and clubs,
And eating houses, restaurants and pubs.
The people are very friendly,
And good hearted are the local gentry.
The buses are not a few,
So you don't stand in a long queue.
The library is very spacious,
And of books very capacious.
The churches cater for the need,
Of Streatham's British bull-dog breed.

W Fred Tabaczynski

THE WEEPING WILLOW

I weep with you my willow friend. Whose branches droop to hang your tears. In forms of leaves. Each slender and long. They reach for the water where your tears flow along. Mine flow in my heart. I feel too your great pain of sorrow and sadness. But your voice can't exchange. Instead you just touch me. Your leaves brush my side. To give me great comfort that no words can describe. I hope that me near brings comfort to you. We weep both together till that day all anew. When these tears from our sadness have washed all away. Our sorrow and sadness for that whole new bright day.

Sandra Brisck

THE KING

This man he is a legend
His voice is so unique

His smile could melt the coldest heart
And make your knees grow weak

People travelled far and wide
Just to hear this legend sing

To all his fans around the world
This man he was the king

Thousands walked around in shock
And many, many cried

For it was such a tragic day
The day that Elvis died

George Dickens

THOUGHTS OF LONDON

Memories come flooding back
Rag and bone men, coal by the sack
Mournful hoots of ships on the Thames
Calling Tower Bridge to open for them.

Horse-drawn carts, the sadness, the fun
Lord Mayor shows, the R100 and one
Methy drinkers at Spitalfields' Church Steeple
The all inspiring St Paul's Cathedral.

Hampstead Heath, tuppence for tea
Hyde Park Corner, 'Who'll vote for me?'
Prince Monalooloo, 'I gotta horse'
Dreams of wealth - we're broke of course.

Whitechapel Library where we'd all meet
Sadlers Wells' Opera, we'd queue for a seat
The boat race day, Henley's regatta,
Losing at Ascot, what did it matter?

Salt beef sandwiches less than a shilling
Guess your weight - who would be willing?
Herrings in barrels, Assenheims ices
Hot chestnut stands and custard slices.

The animal market in old Club Row
This was the London I used to know
This was the London for you and for me
And all those who were born before 1923.

Maria Driffill

ONLY

Only was lonely,
As he stood in the rain,
A face with no features,
A face with no name,
As he walked down the road of warmly lit houses,
Of people with lives and company and togetherness,
As he opened the door,
As only the cold came to greet him,
As no-one was there,
And as no-one called out to him,
As he sat in his chair,
As he fell fast asleep,
As his heart stopped beating,
As his breathing grew weak,
As the smell caught attention,
As the police knocked down the door,
As they brought him out,
And as he was no more,
From beginning to end he was alone,
From cradle to grave all on his own.

Nicola Millwood

One

There was a young girl,
Sitting right there,
With a necklace of pearl,
And a head full of hair,
Where curl after curl,
Was groomed with such care,
And round she would whirl,
As fast as she'd dare,
How well she could twirl,
And with such flair . . .

Where did she go to,
That child so alive,
I know that she grew,
Much older than five,
Now, this is her cue,
To come out of her hive,
'Let's me and you,'
I then softly cry,
Join all anew,
And together we'll jive.

So hand in hand,
We twisted and turned,
Across many lands,
Above tree and fern,
Over sea and sand,
And fire aburn,
We felt mighty grand,
So much to discern,
Now as one we stand,
Wanting more to learn.

Anna Heffron

THERAPY

Your voice on the line
Secret anodyne
I waited so long
My hopes still so strong
My love, it has nowhere to go

Your voice on the line
Like a bottle of wine
Goes straight to my head
With you, in my bed
My love, it has nowhere to go

Your voice on the line
Invisible, divine
Feels like a life-support
Something I should have fought
My love, it has nowhere to go

Fran Pulford

THE TRAMP WITH SPARKLY EYES

From a vulgar alley, that stank of dogs' doings and vomit,
a tattered frame - crumpled as the bag holding the whisky,
shuffled aimlessly into view.
And, reeking of rough living through dirty days,
attracted disgusted looks from passers-by.

Though they, in their purposeful lives,
knew nothing of the tragedy that once came to his door,
he knew he deserved their revolt.
It was his fault, and his choice,
to have nothing but his sparkly eyes.

In these eyes, as in better days,
there was once hope and health.
But now, while his liver screams for mercy,
all that is there in those eyes
is the painful regret of wrong doing
and a vigorous dancing flame that teases his conscience
until he can take no more.

He succumbs to the urge for a swig.

Harsh, scornful memories take residence until,
passed out, he manages to escape.

He jumps from the rim of the bottle,
falling and falling to the bottom,
that is, all too soon, as empty as his soul.
He has found the safety net of numbness,
and has been jumping ever since the fateful night
he jumped from the ledge, away from the fire.

These days he cannot smoke in his cardboard bed,
and since the day his children died
the fire has danced in his eyes.

T L Kelvie

AT A GLANCE

A heartfelt moment.
Stopped and stared.
Glistened in the evening light.
The moon's rays stronger
Than the sun's.
Not as much light
But more depth.
More meaning.
A different meaning to the world
We already knew.

We didn't understand each other.
We didn't know the feelings that existed.
Not passion, not love, not lust,
But a chance to know each other.
Help each other out.

But the moment passed us by
And we grew young.
We'd learnt everything
There was to learn
But couldn't communicate.
Wouldn't.

Walking up the valley
We fell down and missed
The chance.

Now I'm still young.

Mischa Pearlman

MEMORIES

Here again on the same spot I stood years ago,
my memories wandering now, to and fro'.
A lot of things changed over time that has passed,
the people, the places, it's happened so fast.

We had family days at the town's outside pool,
a community place, where I went with my school.
That building, no longer a school, still stands strong,
although all of the laughter of children has gone.

Summer holidays came, much time spent at the fair,
as a young girl I worked on the pedaloes there.
Where a sand pit for children now covers its floor,
and the slot machines stay, but the rides are no more.

But the place that brings most of my life back to me,
is my breakwater post where I stare out to sea.
The fun that I had as I played on the beach,
my mum and my dad never far out of reach.

We swam in bright water, then stood in its glare,
trying hard to make out the wrecks mast in the air.
Many shelters to hide in, our parents to miss,
then later, as teenagers, boyfriends to kiss.

Though the landscape will change and more people will leave,
the sea never alters, it watches us grieve.
It flows on unspeaking through happy and sad,
its water unclear now, what history it's had.

My mind takes me back to the storms, when the sea,
crashed over the boundaries and rush toward me.
I too have moved on now, but with my family,
I will always return here to stare at the sea.

Sally Copeland

IN THE AFTERMATH

Shut off, cut off,
Confusion, delusion.
Closed doors to the open world.

Wondering, pondering,
Re-living, regretting,
Thinking things over and over and over.

Uncertainty, certainly,
Fear, nothing's clear,
The permanent burden of emptiness.

Hoping, but knowing,
It's over, forever.
Nothingness envelopes the nothing you feel.

James Grieve

ISLE OF SHEPPEY

Do you remember Sheppey and the way it used to be?
Going down to the Whitehouse collecting cockles for tea.
Tree climbing in the Glen helped by a length of rope,
Joining in all the hymns at the Minster Band of Hope.

Visiting Sheppey Hospital enquiring of the closure date,
Hope they find a change of mind, before it is too late.
Mrs Durrant's tasty home-made toffees, the very best by far,
When we've never heard of drugs or seen a foreign car.

Cliff pathways up to Leysdown all the wildlife around,
Giant mushrooms in every meadow just waiting to be found.
Visiting Warden Post Office quite near to Warden Bay,
Sadly now no longer in use because of erosion and decay.

The long winding walk with our friends, to visit Harty Ferry,
Having a few of their potent brew, finishing up quite merry.
Planes taking off at Eastchurch to commence a morning flight
The lovely view of Brambledown seen from the 'Sheppey Light'.

The distant view of Elmley with its harvest of autumn gold,
Those very mild Sheppey winters when we never felt the cold.
I hope you've enjoyed reminiscing and before we close our book
If you remember all this, you are much older than you look!

F E M Grimwade

THE VETERINARY VISIT

The old blue door is open wide
While little pets parade inside
I think it looks a little scary
And really feel a little weary
What's all that noise behind the doors
I'm sure I heard a lion's roars
It must be someone with infections
I'm only here for my injections
Oh! how much longer do I wait?
To just find out my awful fate
And then I hear the dreaded text
Come on in! I think you're next

I Ayres

THE BLUE POPPY EFFECT

Sugared by your gaze,
Candy am I.
Brittle enough to
Melt.
Tongue-tip tied in sherbet fizzing over
Bite leaves petals dripping
And I taste the whole of me concentrated
In these lips.
My look drops from your ice-blues,
To your mouth.
Like blue poppies yield in a field
Of sunshine rape.

Amanda Ritson

MY BLESSINGS

I look across the room at my husband.
The man I have known since he was a boy.
We have such a happy life together.
He fills my heart with joy.
We share our ups and we share our downs.
With many smiles and few little frowns.
We have such a wonderful family.
Full of happiness and love.
For all our gracious things in life.
We thank the Lord above.

Penny

LEYSDOWN ON SEA

So elegant stands the Rose and Crown.
Most imposing building in Leysdown.
All the rest look run down shacks,
housing gaming machines and burger snacks.

Blue flag beaches brings much cheer.
Sea is clean and beaches are clear.
Little shops with buckets and spades,
beach balls, toys and eye shades.

Fields and fields of caravans.
Bottled gas and pots and pans.
There is the coastal park
for ball games and fun after dark.

Take a walk for a mile or two.
Fresh sea air, beautiful view.
See big ships aiming for Sheerness Docks.
Pretty girls in summer frocks.

There is quite a lot of sun.
Much scope for plenty of fun.
Leysdown I might say,
very good place for holiday.

R E J Gent

BATTLE STATIONS

Is our hospital still dying?
When so desperately we're trying
To save the services we've got
Downgrading at the K & C
Is so appalling don't you see
So many lives will be at stake
So come on *now* give *us* a break

No children's ward
No baby care
No neo-natal intensive care
Are we prepared to pay the cost
And risk so many being lost

So many people from EK
Will demonstrate along the way
To show support, to show they care
And say let them close it
If they dare!

In the Commons we will fight them
And protest upon our street
For our hospital needs saving
From our bureaucratic fleet

So with a fighting spirit
We'll march upon the street
And let them know they cannot close it
'Cos we the people
Won't be beat

Mark Tann

REASONS TO BE HAPPY

Through unhappy tears, she gazed those fields.
A graceful breeze, on a land that yields
Hungry lambs, so small, so sweet.
A green velvet carpet to protect their feet.
The calm of the sea, the ocean's sway.
The fisherman's boat leaving the bay.
Our sun slips down, slowly out of sight.
The moon takes over to brighten this night.
A cloak falls down and rests on the ground.
Serenity now surrounds this land.
All in all things aren't so bad.
For God's always there with a helping hand.
To glance around she felt truly blessed.
To see mother nature at her best.
She smiled, she was happy, come
what may at the end of a truly
   perfect day.

Sally Carpenter

JUST AS BEFORE

I dreamt I heard you call, siren like.
Through the early morn.
Just as before.
Your gentle footsteps down the hall.
Your perfume drifts through my open door.

I dreamt I felt your touch upon my arm.
Your lips upon my cheek.
Your golden tresses around my shoulders fall.
Alas, if this be dreaming
Then why should I wish to awake at all.

Howard Lucas

EMILY

She'll never wear those Doc Marten boots
Never be seen in *Armani* suits
She'll never be a Brownie or a Girl Guide
Never be a Bridesmaid, never be a Bride

She'll never go to 'Big School', never learn to write
Never tie her shoe-laces, never fly a kite
She'll never go to *Disneyland* or visit Alton Towers
Never make a daisy-chain or pick a bunch of flowers

She'll never be forgotten, never slip from mind or heart
She'll never be an 'extra', *Leading lady* was her part
She'll never cause a family row, never let you down
Never break a promise, she'll never cause one frown

Dear wee Emily, so brightly shone your star
Loved by both your brothers, sister too and by Ma and Pa
Now in Heaven, creating *havoc* ('cos that's what Em's about)
And adored by everybody up there, of that I have no doubt

She'll never wear those Doc Marten boots
Never be seen in *Armani* suits
But this dear little lady will *always* be there
Memories of a joyous short life are all ours to share

David Hallwood

UNKNOWN REGIONS

Strange eyes that look and see
Where none have seen
Strange ears that hear
Where none have heard
Strange feet that walk
Where none dare tread
And hands that clasp
And feel and touch

Strange footprints in the sands of time
Forever there by man unseen
No man can go to see, to hear
To walk the paths of planets rare
Were I go to see and hear
Would I go and see in fear
The earth, the sky, the moon, the stars
From the distant red of planet Mars

Or Jupiter its colours bright
Would I sit there through the night
And wonder at its serenity
Should I find some life on Mars
What would I do there among the stars
Would I see friend or foe
Would I stay or go

But Earth its beauty I would miss
Never again to feel the kiss of sun-drenched rain
Or smell its fresh cool air
And though I wonder at the stars
The planets Jupiter and Mars
I am content for them to see
One day in eternity.

Una Daniels

Last Love

A year ago the falling snow lay deep in the white winter of my soul
In bitterness I shunned the fire and embraced the heartless cold
Alone I slept, alone I rose, alone clutched like a straw
Yet drowning in my all alone, in my life that lived no more.

She came to me as spring trickled down and green draped the earth like robes
A sister to my loneliness, as tender in her beauty as the petals of a rose
And I saw her dreams, and I knew her heart and all her soul laid bare
So that old fell away, and grey fell away and ugly was once again fair.

The summer came and endless days of lush and green and grow
Bathed her in hazy splendour beneath its gentle sunny glow
Soon the fields were full, my heart was full from the rich harvest of her smile
And colours came, and simple came until my eyes saw like a child's.

Then autumn clouds came down like shrouds and her soul was in her deep brown eyes
A well of tears for all the years she was not by my side
And in the ache of my heart, I felt the depth of her pain
As she grieved for the young love, crying out for the lost love which could never, never come again.

And now the year has turned again and the wind carries winter's chill
But the cold is not so bitter and the storms inside are still
So that I'll go on, and we'll go on until the life in us has ceased
In the wisdom that we learnt so late that only love brings peace.

Tony Skidmore

STREETWISE WOMAN

it was a mystery to her, but the fight did commence.
yet there were no soldiers to stand in the trench.
it wasn't a battle of the violent kind.
she was fighting for her life. she put the past behind.

a long time ago she heard a distant call.
she chose to ignore it, but now the writing's on the wall.
twenty years old, but she looks like thirty.
spending most of her life living grubby and dirty.

now the times have changed, the tables have turned.
she's lived the experience, and now she's learned.
the clown may smile, the joker may laugh.
yet each of them walk down the same footpath.

she's been scarred for life with no compensation.

the streetwise woman.

Shaun Edwards

DEDICATED TO MY HUSBAND

I wanted to grow old with you
I thought we had it made
But now you're gone
To a better place
Memories won't fade
You made me laugh
You made me cry
You made me want to sigh
I loved you lots
You tied me in knots
When your life passed you by
God took you away
Where good folks stay
To a place where nobody's seen
You left a big hole
Where you once were
Now emptiness is all that seems

D Sampford

GENTLE APRIL BREEZE

Oh gentle April breeze that comes -
That comes to warm, to touch and end the winter fast.

Oh gentle April breeze
That comes again
To wake the blossom from its sleep,
As creatures small from woodland creep.

Oh gentle April breeze awake -
Awake to breathe, caress and paint with pallet green,
The hues and subtle shades so long unseen.

Oh gentle April breeze that comes -
That comes but lingers less
And passes softly through
With still a hint of winter in your breath.

Richard Francis

The Violent Sea

When storm clouds bow to winter's call
That bends to every whim
And sturdy ships that wilt and fall
Have succumbed to nature's sin

New found waters vest with wrath
In search of easy game
And fickle seas from wanton graft
Unleash their ravished pain

As rapturous thunder screams with glee
And bellows with strong voice
A violent call that marks the sea
And has no certain choice

Lightning shows like shattered glass
And cracks amongst the sky
And raindrops fall from distance far
To flood a land once dry

Sailors cower on battered decks
From spitting venom waves
And bodies litter deep sea wrecks
From violent seas depraved

D H Pepperrell

HATFIELD HEATH

First Mr Dix, then Mr Foster
Learning with them the children prosper
We said our goodbyes to the Trinity Hall
Completely rebuilt, before it could fall

Four pubs, two butchers, a cobblers too
They even campaigned for a public loo
Poles put down to protect the green
Signs by the shops must not be seen

Fun run, dog show and catering tent
The festival became an annual event
Side shows and displays, there's plenty to see
You can even sample a home-made cream tea

The playschool's been running for a many a year
Fun and laughter, but sometimes a tear
The Waggon and Bucks are names in the past
The houses in Willow Green are going up fast

From Chinese to Thatchers to Hunter's Meet
You're spoilt for choice of places to eat
Sarbir's developments continue to grow
Sometimes the Heath Players put on a show

Terry has moved from veg to papers
The Parish Council continue their capers
For 50 years both man and boy
To live in this village has been a joy!

David Brown

FOLLOW ME

If you are looking for love
Come follow me
I will show you all the wonders of love
there is to see

I will make you feel
you have never been loved before
you will feel all the emotions
of love
that you have never felt before

So come follow me
I'll show you what I mean
You will never look back
and you will always love me

Rachel Wake

FAIRIES

The *fairies* come at night I'm told
When children are asleep
They play with toys of children small
For them it is a treat

They live in woods in shady trees
With birds and squirrels too
They use the leaves to make their dress
And stalks to make their shoes

When night time falls the *fairies* meet
To visit all the toys
They haven't any of their own
Like lucky girls and boys

So when you go to bed at night
And put your toys away
Leave out the ones that aren't too big
So *fairies* they can play

Jane Bye

I Am

I am the day
you are the sun
I am the party
you are the fun
I am the summer
and you are the breeze
I am the lock
that you pick with ease

I am the night
and you are my moon
I am the medicine
you are the spoon
I am the winter
and you are the snow
I am the seed
you make me grow
I am all you want me to be
the sky, the earth, the land and the sea
We are nothing without the other
The world God created is nature's mother

S Went

AN I AM POEM

I am the wonder of the rainbow.
The happiness in your eyes.
I am the breeze on a hot day
The kind words your best friend may say.
I am the tinsel on your Christmas tree.
I am the silence at night.
The victory for your favourite club.
I am the No. 1 song by your favourite band.
I am the stranger who gave you their hand.
I am the colour in a great piece of art.
I am the love that is in your heart.

Emma Cass

HEAVEN AND EARTH

For you ask 'What is it
This place called earth,
That man lives and works
And eventually dies upon?'
A place to find the wonders of life:
Babies, bubbles, flowers and trees;
Make bearable the struggles, the strife
Of this world we call earth.

And now the years advance you ask
'What is it that place called heaven?'
No-one knows for sure - we can only surmise
That it's the same as that called earth,
With babies, bubbles, flowers, trees;
But without the struggles, the strife -
A place to give thanks on our knees
For His world we call heaven.

Jennifer Vrahimis

OUR MEN IN THE GATE

They fall one upon another
To lay in their own silence on the grey stones.
We had walked that same road
To turn and watch them finally be still.
Unlike our fellows, we shall go back
Reflecting on unfinished lives.

Dark clouds throw cold rain relentlessly
To wash the flat unmoving forms,
Now trampled by returning feet of those who live -
But also remember
Their vibrant intensity of life.

Left to rest in the raw elements of time,
Their damaged forms fade white
As life's colour drains away with the rain,
Flowing red rivulets in the trenches of the glistening cobbles.

A last lone poppy flutters through the top of the Menin Gate
Drifting silently to join its fallen comrades,
Wet and mutilated on the ground.
Dry petals lifted away by mourners
Are carried homeward
In memory of those who will lie forever in foreign soil.

J A Taft

INSIDE ST THOMAS' GATE

She stood alone -
How hard for her to speak.
And, as she murmured
Of her grief
A teardrop fell;
And strained my heart as well.

Her grief was mine -
Just for a time
She would release
That moment gone;
Until her empty
Heart moved on.

I, a stranger to her,
Meeting in that space,
Before the cold, set
In her heart again.
I should have known,
Her sun had set, too soon.

The cause was lost -
Long before I
Crossed her path -
I tried to grasp;
That time we shared . . .
Inside St Thomas' Gate.

Donald James Munday

LINES WRITTEN IN MEMORY OF A PROPOSAL

There's an old sea-wall
By the coast-line of Amalfi
Where the waves rush.

And the old cold stones
Listen quietly to the evening
And the wind's hush.

And the season's paint is peeling
Where the sun once fell
And warmed us.

C F Iggulden

THE RELUCTANT GARDENER

We moved from the town to this haven of peace,
A wilderness where time seemed to cease.
It was our new home in our last years of life
Only us to look after it, just me and the wife.

This haven of joy for wildlife unknown
The old nest in the tree, the birds long since flown.
Tangled weeds and long dead flowers
To clear this garden would take us hours.

I mourned the little creatures that we had disturbed
But she used her trowel and strimmer unperturbed.
As we used fork and spade I thought it a sin
To part the earth and reveal their cosy homes within.

They scuttle away in panic, at this sudden light of day
But I the reluctant gardener just drop my fork and walk away.

The garden work is over now, so we just rest awhile,
As she rests contented, on her face a smile.
Weeds and brambles gone the garden now looks tidy and neat,
And I relax with the insects back in their homes beneath our feet.

David John Gaywood

SOUNDS IN THE SILENCE

The sounds of horses' hooves
Pulling the gun carriage
Break the silence, punctured too
By the tears and sobs which freely flow.

The footsteps of the soldiers
Accompanying the silence
Vie now with a lone piper
Playing a lament
As the Abbey's bells
Toll out their muffled peal.

Inside the sanctuary
There is solemn quiet
While choirboys' voices
Soar above a world of grief.
Outside, under the still
And leaf-covered trees,
The thousands repeat in muted unison
The 'Our Father',
Then listen to the strains of
'I am the resurrection and the life.'

Eyes turn soon to watch
The draped catafalque
Placed in a sombre hearse
For its long journey
To a green corner of Northamptonshire.

As the mourning crowds applaud
And crown Diana with petal power
We sense the fragrance of their acts
Will haunt our memories
For the many decades yet to be.

Brian Frost

I'D LIKE TO BE A KITTEN!

I'd like to be a kitten
So that you can play with me,
I'd like to play in boxes and move them all about,
I'd like some more attention I hardly get any,
I'd like to be a kitten and nobody's stopping me.

Jenny Lines (11)

JUST FOR NOW

Curates crawl, babies bawl,
High strung lanterns tend to fall,
But here and now, where I am stood,
Life is good,
It's Hollywood.

So let it rain, endure your pain
Or guilt struck wounds or mental strain,
Look at the leaves that never fight,
Believe tonight,
They've got it right.

Yes just for now, denounce the vow,
Absorb the lie that I endow,
Greet terror with a gaudy kiss,
Make virgins hiss,
We all need this.

A touch of blade, of devil's trade,
Of seething venom lemonade,
Let scarlet wings engulf the skin,
Let's be akin,
Let's suck some sin.

The morning sun will make them run:
Those monsters who drank tears for fun,
But we can write,
That on that night,
We held their hands and praised the Fight,
We spat and swore and stubbed the Light,
'Twas wrong,
But just for now, it's right.

Patrick Farrelly

THE LESSON

Bells ring,
Children run,
The day done,
New life begun.

Clocks tick,
Time runs,
Adults rush,
The pace too much.

Lessons past and present,
To be learnt by us all,
The truth hard on the person,
Oh! But the joy of it all.

Will we ever know what drives us,
Fate or fortune?
Love or hate?
The sadness and the gladness,
Of what we've known before,
Leaves us standing,
Alone with ourselves,
Reflecting the past,
And the importance of now,
The real lesson for us all.

Helen Tingley

DYING LOVE

The floorboards creak and the
noise grows louder.
Shouting, screaming and crying
comes from the floor above.
Why do they always argue?
Their love is becoming like a dying fire.

Dawn is drawing nearer.
Silence hangs like clouds around the room,
Now there is not a sound,
but my own breathing and the birds outside.
I listen, but all is quiet, peaceful.
Almost as if the world is dead!

Samantha Gout (12)

VALENTINE FOR CHARLIE

You wait for me
to free you from your prison,
wait patiently at dawn
dark eyes glisten

Soft, softly yielding
the hollow behind your ears,
bury my face in your nape
to calm your quivering fear.

Dodge and weave in the garden,
escaping the invisible foe -
skittishly, playful and leaping
you earth brown, hay scented doe.

You bunch in my lap,
lie, stretched on the floor -
nose always ticking
but can't give more.

We are both middle aged now -
though you do not sigh -
Once, I owned rabbit lined gloves,
Charlie . . .
        how could I?

S F Burley

UNTITLED

Have you ever been stuck for a word?
I mean, isn't it absurd,
There I was in full flow
And suddenly . . . oh!
Dear oh dear, it was on the tip!
(now doesn't this really take the pip),
Of my tongue.

This really is silly, dearie me,
I am sure you will agree,
I was just saying that
I had it off pat.
I mean! . . . You know! . . . Of course you do!
It's always clear to folks like you
What's wrong.

It's so sad and I'm forlorn
My word's completely gorn,
So I must just admit
That my muse has flit
Suzy, 'scuse me, I must whiz,
That's the state in which I is,
So long!

Martin Harris Parry

MEMORIES

I've started to reflect over the changing years.
Feeling joyous and laughing, and sad moments for tears.
There's been men in space, men to the moon.
Guess, we'll be bussing there, one day soon.
Spice Girls, Bros, and Backstreet Boys
and those loveable, big-eyed Teletubby toys.
Gone are Tibs and Rover, in are Cyber Pets.
No more expensive trips to the vets!
That exciting Lottery on Saturday nights.
Families at tellies praying their numbers are right.
Always remembering sad times as Dunblane.
Grief in our hearts will always remain.
Could we ever forget our Princess Di.
All over the world, heads low, did we cry!
Our saddest day was to lose baby Abigail.
Only hours old, she died, so frail.
May you rest in peace little one.
We'll see you again, when our day is done.
Maybe for now memories are through.
Next for us all the Millennium is due.

Maggie Ford

SPRING SONG

Spring is in the air,
And with it comes the moans,
As out of hibernation
Come the roadworks with their cones.

Holes are everywhere.
They blossom overnight.
Just like weeds, they prosper,
And spread their evil blight.

For weeks they're unattended,
No-one knows why they are there.
Then overnight, mysteriously,
They simply disappear!

Geraldine Foy

Cursed With A Minor Talent

Cursed with a minor talent
Lost between the head and the heart
I wanna spray my name on the wall of fame
All in the name of art
Vaguely unforgettable
Brilliantly uninspired
Try to be true to the work that you do
If you wanna be admired

Cursed with a minor talent
Stuck between the cream and the crap
I wanna fix my face in the marketplace
If only I can find a gap
Pick me up and dust me down
Don't leave me on the shelf
I want the world to love me
As much as I love myself

Cursed with a minor talent
Caught between the good and the great
I wanna cut me a slice of something nice
Before it gets too late
In pictures words and music
I ply my stock in trade
Look at me - I'm not like you
This is what I made.

Vic Lime

DARK ROOMS

Behind our eyes lie darkrooms
A focus on our youth
A welcome candle brings light to the darkest of
rooms
And sometimes a dancing shadow
Will show a slight glimmer of truth.

I welcome you a burning candle
To my darkest room
Your lingering presence throws light into a place
That can be quieter than an ancient tomb.

Within our society the masses are indifferent
To those who cry
While being so accepting of those who so
Readily lie.

Being let down by the thoughts and attitudes
Of others can leave us feeling as if
Our minds are slowly decomposing even though
Our bodies are drenched with the spirit of life.

These thoughts and feelings ebb from
Within my darkest rooms
And sometimes I wonder whether the
Realisation of my whole being has brought
An unwanted doom
But yet again there are many burning candles
That will light my darkest rooms.

K McDonagh

YOUR VALENTINE?

Last year you said she had the works
Red roses, chocolates and a card,
Feb 14th is here again,
Will you do the same?

Will you buy her flowers?
Will you give a card?
Do you, because you feel you should
Or is your love deep down still there?

This year you did the same,
Roses, chocolates and a card,
Dinner, earrings and a bracelet too,
But what did she give you?

No card for you, no smile, no kiss,
No dinner and no love,
No hearts, no flowers, no special thanks,
No look to say she cares.

Disappointment is a sad old word,
It does not tell enough of what you want
And what you get
And what you are dreaming of.

SQ

THE CHANGE OF TIME

How I remember the days gone by -
When we were children, my brothers and I -
After school each day - we would play
Outside our house, in our own sweet way -
Mothers and fathers, or on an old wooden truck,
Sit on the step, didn't notice the muck -
Sometimes, a friend would own a bike
'Oh let's have a go' 'OK - If you like.'
Then Mum would call us, in for tea
We sat at the table - no tele -
Switch on the wireless for children's hour -
Have a quick wash, we hadn't a shower.
Too cold in the kitchen, to stay out there -
Get back for a go on the old rocking chair.
We then hit the wall and Mum has a shout!
One of us ends up, getting a clout!
So off up the stairs and so to bed -
In the winter - it's freezing, something we dread -
Ice on the windows, our breath in the air -
Fold up your clothes on the bedside chair -
'Don't talk, get to sleep' our mum would say -
'Have you said your prayers?'
What a perfect day.

Minnie Dann

Elemental Experience (Water, Fire, Air and Earth)

Flow to me
Gentle waves of feeling
Guide my passion with depths profound
Envelop my limbs
Gentle waves of feeling
Make me aware of the smallest sound

Dance for me
Wild flames of amber
Warm my body to passionate heat
Fan my heart
Wild flames of amber
To your rhythm let me strongly beat

Fly to me
Sweet breezes of love
On a warm wind, fragile and light
Linger awhile
Sweet breezes of love
Fill my head with wondrous delight

Stabilise me
Live pulses of earth
To feel your substance hard and strong
Ground my direction
Live pulses of earth
Lead me to where I belong.

Janis Huntley

DEEP LOSS

A sea of darkness, the clouded moon,
Knowing my heart will forget you soon,
Sombre moaning like the howling of cats,
Time stood still like a pausing smile.

You are my life, my heart, my song,
My smile when things went wrong,
The air I breathe, the food I eat, the water I drink,
I never knew such loss as this could cause such hurt.

Although my soul stands rigid with pain,
I hear you calling again and again,
You are my life, my heart, my song,
But, for me my life *must* carry on.

Elaine Coldwell (16)

Untitled

Loves' gentle missal I heard say
Was written in the breeze of a summer's day
With gentle hands it holds us, cares and enfolds us
And upon my youthful heart love's gentle hand did lay

In rays of yellow sunshine I found my spirit caught
I sought them in trees and fields and wooden cart wheels
That stand then move like time
At the end of the day the shadows stay
They increase with the sun's decline

My love and I did sleep among rays of golden light
The exchange of love between us held us together tight
To my own person I took qualities she did possess
And she took same of mine and then our love the gods did bless.

S Wickes

SHATTERED DREAM

I lost sight of my dream
Or so it would seem
The years flew away
Grains of sand in my hand
The world grew so small
There was nothing at all

Once I knew songs
Once I would dance
But I knew in one glance
I'd lost every chance
The laughter once mine
Was lost for all time
When I turned round and saw
There was nothing at all.

Empty chairs empty tables
Empty bottles of wine
The dream that I held
Was no longer mine
The world grew so small
Now there's nothing at all.

Linda Walker

Duty Calls

You wouldn't believe me if I told you,
Of some of the sights I have seen.
Just where some people wash themselves,
In order to make sure they are clean.

Look here comes Tracey right now,
Every day like clockwork you see her.
First she undresses and then she spends,
An hour and a half by the mirror.

Finally she steps into the shower,
And adjusts the water to her liking.
With arms raised high behind her head,
That's a beautiful pose that she's striking.

Now it's my turn as she reaches out,
And scoops me up from my dish.
I hope I get the usual treatment
There's no harm in having a wish.

It looks like the wait is over,
It's going to be happening now I can tell.
Being rubbed in all her private places,
Ooh I serve my mistress well.

My heart begins to calm itself,
As I'm put back in my tray.
I watch Tracey rub herself dry,
And look forward to another day.

Still in my heart there is sadness,
As with each wash I tend to shrink.
We don't get to last that long you see,
There'll be someone else in my place next week.

Robert Wassell

MY DREAM

We all have dreams of that I am sure,
I had one that was so very pure.
To travel the world and make people smile
Would be the answer and make life worthwhile.

With British Airways my answer did come;
Dressed in my blue my life had begun.
To make customers happy as they travel by air
Was my answer completely and they had no cares.

Our company motto is surely the best;
We all love our work so we don't take a rest.
To please all the people, yes out on the street
It gives some folk headaches but to us it's a treat.

Enzo Gizzi

Not Long To Live?

Time's rapid passage moves silent and unseen,
Though life seems hardly yet begun;
And weekends pass so fast in pastimes or in dream.
For each of us, how few are yet to run?

Tristan Cooper

A MAN WHO LOVED WOMEN

A man who loved women,
That was my father
But one above all other.
Denial became an illicit affair
Which convention could not contain.
Their love caused much grief and pain
In the midst of their joy.
Over the years they yearned to be
United in marriage.
When the moment came
It was too late.
A lifetime of love
Snatched away by cruel irony
That one above all other
Was, sadly, not my mother.

Lesley Gooden

ODE TO THE BUNG

Set between the sea and land
On neither hill nor shingle strand
Its unpretentious charms unsung
Far from Reigate lies the Bung.

A world away from Surrey life
And middle-class and work and strife
Romnia beckons, cares outflung
Bohemian rhapsody - the Bung.

Here lifetime memories are made
Parental 'no's' defer to 'yes'
Simple childhood games are played
From Fairlight's cliffs to Dungeness.
A kite to fly and lunch delayed
The siren call of the Bung's caress
To sleep or swim, the choice is made
Of idle fun or idleness.

On stormy night or gentle days
Its simple pleasures mildly praise.
Unstring the bow that life has strung
Relax, chill out - enjoy the Bung.

Golden walls and ceiling blue
Spiders dancing in the loo.
At summer's end, the last lark's sung
Memories linger of the EP's bung.

John Gooden

SUMMER'S GONE TERRY

Your life's gone down the drain Terry,
Like the apple jelly it got spoiled.
For days I nurtured that stuff.
Boiled it, stirred it and strained it
And then in two seconds it was all over.
Instead of summer deep golden in jars,
Old blood brown fingers
Had sucked the warm winds away
Down the drain.

They took away the lilac days.
Took the bright spring petals served by the bee.
Took the naive little nipples of first apple and
The honeyed mellowings of red and gold.
Just a few seconds too many, a few rogue cells and
Then bang
Your life's a gonner Terry like a rotten apple,
Splat!

You were a funny little man.
A funny little life sucked away.
Yours was a family though!
Gossiping on doorsteps half the night.
Laughs and squabbles galore
And kids in and out all the time.
Never a quiet moment when you could contemplate
What was coming.
Fish papers and fags all over the place
Along with slippered feet and dogs.
They were altogether round the bed when you went though.
With you they were Terry 'til the end
'Til you were pulled down the chute last summer.

Sheila Rabbetts

PARADOX

Extreme addiction to the breath of life,
exploring the avenue of discovery,
This is the road to recovery,

Eliminating time to soothe this battered soul,
to pray expulsion of sad memories,
mellowing with the passage of the years,

Each hour, day to be a new experience,
knowing eventually the satisfaction of our being,
that we have journeyed through our mistakes and misfortunes,

Are we not here for a limited space of time,
to cherish all living things, to give of ourselves,
to the greater peace of mankind,
enveloping the love so much needed?

Barbara Anslow

BREATHING

Silence is not the absence of sound . . .
It is the breathing of creation
When human noise has ceased

Restoration of earth's movement
When man has paused
His buzzing membranes still
To feel again the harmony he disrupts

Leaf fall, twig break, water lap
A tuning of the ear to distance
The half heard receding echo of a stillness

A gentle breeze of cooling quiet to the skin
Becoming transparent, an osmosis of calm
Passing through till . . . self ceases to be separate

A release, a lightness, a lifting
A floating in the singing silence of earth's music
A tremor as the anchor of self . . . lets go and weight is gone

Rising and lifting now only within the breathing silence
that orchestrates creation's life
Above the roofs and trees, above the sleeping town

Dark shape of hills and trees, the lighter arc
of distant horizons marking man's boundaries
And, high above, the shining stars caught in the net of night

Release the fear of letting go of all familiar things
The known, the understood, all that can be framed
within the human mind to give us comfort, safety

The breathing is no longer yours now for you have become
Leaf fall, twig break, water lap
Alien to yourself but free to join a greater harmony

For silence is not the absence of sound . . .
It is the breathing of creation
When human noise has ceased.

Keith Donachie

WAR POEM

Down here, here in the ground,
Am I safe? Am I sound?
Who knows where I am?
Can anyone see me?
Who'd want to be me?
This war won't end,
I haven't a friend,
They've all died,
But I survived.
The sky's so blue,
Yet I feel so grey.
Oh, war, please go away.

Andrea Foulkes

'HONEY'S' COMING HOME

For two long years, I've been alone,
Without a soul to call my own,
A telephone, a word or two,
The first I heard or knew of you,
A kindly voice, a friendly tone,

And *'Honey' might* come home.

You came from somewhere, no-one knew,
A tired old lady, frightened too,
Strange hands and smells, you couldn't see,
And now I knew you needed me

And *'Honey' could* come home.

A gentle paw, a quiet purr,
And arms around your soft warm fur.
A few more words, a form to sign,
A little while and you'll be mine.

And *'Honey's coming* home.

A fire warm, a bed beside,
A saucer full, no need to hide,
A hasty ride and journey's end.
With lots of love for you my friend.

And *'Honey's* home.

Terry

HALLOWE'EN?

Children come knocking at the door
You know it's Hallowe'en once more
And as they call out 'Trick or treat!'
Who knows what strangers they will meet?

Say 'No!' to 'Trick and Treat' this year
Reduce the risk of harm or fear
To older folks who live alone;
Children from hazards widely known

But do remember All Hallow's Day
Rejoice in that, 'cos that's OK
Jesus is knocking at your door
His 'trickless treat' - life evermore!

Charlie Keenan

HAVING KNOWN YOU FROM AFAR

Having known you,
those fleeting moments,
that beauty,
that you are.

Observing you,
from afar,

Losing myself
to your smile;
your laughter,
sends my spirit to soar.

Just moments,
watching the muse,
intense in your creativity.

The path of the broken heart,
that I have endured,

Now seems worth the enduring;
within those fleeting moments,
having known you
from afar.

Mark Dunn

THE DRESS

I bought a dress from a charity shop
And wondered what I'd got.
The dress seemed to have a life of its own.
The zip broke; the buttons were prone
To fall off, even before I got it home.

I reluctantly tried it on
But it was much too long.
The dress came out where I went in
So I put it into the dustbin.

When Mrs Mopp came to clean
She found the dress and said she was keen
To have the gown, adding
'I'll take it to a charity shop I know in town.'

Helen Cronin

Atlas In A Suit

Come down, you fool!
What do you think you're doing?
It's not a crime to cry
Yet you hold back everything
Like Atlas in a suit
You carry the world around
But it cares not for you
Won't you come back to the ground?

Is it love? Is it money?
Is it the never-ending unknown?
I can empathise, I've been there
I know what you are going through
A plate glass window called life
Well pull up your socks, get a grip

What is it? What's so funny?
You want to be left alone
Well you always were, I don't care
I thought you were wise, thought you knew
No, stop, put down the knife
And let's go through it bit by bit

It's a puzzle, I know
It's a gamble in other ways
Sometimes it couldn't get better
Sometimes it's the worst days
And you know it's all pointless
There is no worth in trying
The good guys never get to live
So I think I'll join you in dying.

Leigh Hunt

BARBED WIRED HARD DRIVE

A brain bound in barbed wire.
The hard drive hums but, there's no redraw.
Man works mechanically, methodically, obediently,
Patiently waiting for Life.

World thrusts herself through an open window,
She tempts, teases, caresses.
Her outstretched slender fingers offer release,
Man wants to taste something new on his numbed palate.
In awe, he is seduced.

World pulls man into her - he sees,
Sees what would have danced before his strangled eyes -
On his bed of death.

Missed.
Peaks shrouded in satin,
Thunderous tempers and warm summer sighs,
Her impenetrable heart, fit to be tackled,
Her inviting oceans, their immeasurable depths,
Her deserts of golden countless curves.

Man is smitten,
He embraces,
His brain bleeds but is free,
The hard drive redraws, finally.
It reveals Life.

J A Gill

Hope

Cold and alone on the battlefield I stand
The fear and the pain
Of the long gone dead
Smouldering buildings
Smashed bodies
Ruined minds,
The price we pay is steep
The hope has gone
The hope is here
Psychedelic swirls of
Blood in my mind.
The noise of silence
Stuns my senses
I need the hope
The hope has gone
The blackness of my soul
Wells up in waves
What has happened?
What has gone?

Sue Calvert

THE NOW

Stop the clocks,
hold back the hands,
keep time waiting . . .
for a second, a minute,
an hour long day,
until such a moment has passed away.

Stand still,
breathe in the now,
see your feet on solid ground,
stay a while watching,
as others blindly rush around.

Think not of tomorrow,
dwell, not long in the past,
seize these precious second moments,
before time catches . . . fast.

C Leith

Colour Of Day

Colour of day
        Colour of night,
Shades of dark
        Shades of light,
All true gifts
        Are given free,
All laid out
        For you and me,
So make the most
        Of every day,
Choose the colour,
        Not the grey.

Christine Ashworth

THE OLD WALL

I helped build the wall that stood outside the door . . .
and saw the first brick put in place.
Then watched 'cross the years as it mellowed with age . . .
and saw the same wear on Pop's face.

It changed very slow and I never did see
the mark of those years till the end.
They'd both stood so strong and protected us true,
With no sign of crack or a bend.

But age takes its toll and with greatest regrets,
Our old wall broke down deep inside.
And that's when I saw that my 'Dear Pop' had aged . . .
And as the wall broke . . . so he died.

T J Martin

JUST A WORD IN PASSING

Learn all you can while life skips along
It passes so quickly, so much can go wrong.
Keep a fair standard and a straight back,
Don't be afraid to admit what you lack.
Evenly proportion all that you give
Seven sins are a must as you learn to live.
Time is a healer, a worry so short,
Humour and conscience cannot be bought,
Take heed, learn your lessons along life's way,
You may need to practice them one fine day.
Old heads on young shoulders cannot be
But remember God helps you as well as me.

E Fisher

DIMINISHING HOPE

With the bowing of the sun
I feel the inevitable
Slowly but not reluctantly happening.

As darkness finally prevails
I am left with nothing
But the emptiness.

Abandon. The word rings in my ears
Sounding so alone and cold
And suddenly I know
I am also alone.

The fading warmth
That has continued for so long
Is no longer there
And I know I must look elsewhere.

Ghazala Rashid

Where Is My Heart?

My heart's in the woodlands, among the green branches,
dappled with sunlight and free as a bird.
Trees ever holding their arms out to greet me,
Was it their voices in dreams that I heard?

The shades in the green woods of nature, I wonder
just how I would paint them, if only my hand
could colour and store them to savour in winter
the wonders I see, but can scarce understand.

Why should we not be as free as the breezes
that blow cross the meadow and over the hill.
'Come with us - run with us' joyfully calling,
'Into the green woods and wander at will.'

If only the body was free as the spirit,
but chained to our benches and desks evermore.
Still, deep in my heart the woodlands are calling
'Come to us, come - before summer is o'er.'

Ruth M Davies

SUNDAY PEACE

A quiet shaded tree lined path
Birds gently singing through still air
Small dogs are chasing flying sticks
As walks and fun their owners share

Grandma and Grandad slowly stroll
A father with a pram walks by
With smiling nod and kindly word
At sound of a new baby's cry

A whirring noise of turning wheels
As cyclists quickly peddle past
While onto deep and dappled lake
Small shining jewels the sunbeams cast

Gleaming blackbird with orange beak
Stands tamely by a picnic spread
While mother duck keeps gentle watch
As ducklings peck some fresh-thrown bread

The sun so warm peeps through green leaves
Making the ground a mottled place
Cow parsnip grows beneath broad boughs
Like collars of fine hand-made lace

As evening slowly settles down
The sound of children's voices cease
Blackbird returning to its nest
Day ends with such calm Sunday peace.

Olive Martin

SIMPLE PLEASURES

Pouring rain;
under umbrella huddled;
river raging,
o'erflowing its banks,
ducks distracted
by wintry frost;
child concealed
beneath plastic covers;
single figure
shivering slowly whilst
throwing bread
to grateful birds.
Sunshine distant,
hard to beckon,
rain falls still
in river's way.
Child kicks happy,
contented, smiling,
looking through his
'window' pane.
Time to go now,
back home safely,
dry and warm
in arms enfolded.
Gently snoozing,
cocooned together.
Single thought in
woman's mind;
'This is happiness'.

Kate Smith

TO JANE

You came in the summer of my life
To cherish and to hold.
Many years have long since passed
And winter's wind blows cold.

I knew your love would pass unchanged
Along the way we strode,
So I thank you for sharing
Life's long rocky road.

Your face, now etched with life,
Shows beauty, pain, love and strife,
Changing, yet unchanged to me,
A prize, a jewel so fine.
How wondrous the day
I made thy body mine.

Barbara Jane Richardson

BIRD

I awake to a bright and eager
Sunday morning and
open a tin of Arthur.
The cats scamper at its sound
and tails erect, beg the
door open.

On the patio lay a tiny scrap
of shivering life, oblivious
to its plight as
it huddles in feathered misery
next to the Tesco
growbag.

I collect and cradle this child
in my giant alien hands
and feel its fear
course through my body.
Misguidedly I try to calm
it with a clumsy finger.

The cats lope eagerly as
I make dew feet in the
pristine lawn and under
the stony gaze of a gnome
I entrust this life to
a high yew tree.

All day Mother screeches
alarm and amongst the
noise and safe cacophony
all is well. but red evening
brings purring cats and a
garden of loud silence.

Archie Wilson

OUR EDEN

What if this is our Eden?
What if I've found our paradise lost?
The time we spend together
Being ourselves to each other,
When we are happy
Or when we're depressed,
There is always life,
There is always love.

What if this is our Eden?
What we thought we'd lost?
Paradise for eternity
And peace forever more;
The gift of life,
Of love
Of light,
When we are ourselves.

Whatever we may believe,
Whoever we follow,
Remember,
We are alive,
Let's recapture our paradise lost.

William Hudson-Jones

DEATH VISITS

Firelight flickers fill this empty room
Warmth reaching but not quite felt,
Shadows play, can't bear to look
I sit, frozen-hearted, rooted to this spot
Willing dawn to save me once more.
My body aches for what I once knew
A stranger to myself, so much change
Pain all consuming, jagged, raw,
Cutting, twisting, like Satan's claw
Screams and howls fill my dreams
Grey shapes mocking with their presence
I try to run but can't turn away
The proverbial rabbit in the headlights
Rigid with fear, all sense of time gone
Waiting, resigned, ready.
Come for me, take me with you
It's my time now, I am no longer afraid
Take me with you, I feel no pain,
I'm finished here, I know you see that,
Your angry shadow tormenting me
Always tormenting in my empty room
I'm ready for you now, I won't light the fire
I'll lie here and wait for as long as it takes,
Only please, make it quick!

Belinda Lonie

INFORMATION

We hope you have enjoyed reading this book - and that you will continue to enjoy it in the coming years.

If you like reading and writing poetry drop us a line, or give us a call, and we'll send you a free information pack.

Write to :-
**Anchor Books Information
1-2 Wainman Road
Woodston
Peterborough
PE2 7BU
(01733) 230761**